Little Writers

EMERGENT PRIMARY WRITING ACTIVITIES

by Linda Lew Dollard

FEARON TEACHER AIDS

Executive Editor: Jeri Cipriano

This Fearon Teacher Aids product was formerly manufactured and distributed by American Teaching Aids, Inc., a subsidiary of Silver Burdett Ginn, and is now manufactured and distributed by Frank Schaffer Publications, Inc. FEARON, FEARON TEACHER AIDS, and the FEARON balloon logo are marks used under license from Simon & Schuster, Inc.

© Fearon Teacher Aids
A Division of Frank Schaffer Publications, Inc.
23740 Hawthorne Boulevard
Torrance, CA 90505-5927

ISBN: 1-56417-859-5

4 5 6 7 8 9   TCS   01 00 99 98

The Write Start

Are you implementing or adding to a whole language program in your school? If so, the reproducibles in this book will be easy for you to adapt to your classroom. The teacher notes preceding each section will help you set the tone for encouraging children to approach writing in a playful and experimental way. You'll find that children who participate in these activities will develop a variety of writing skills that will enable them to achieve independence in written communication.

CONTENTS

PICTURE REVIEWS

Children's artwork is a natural extension of stories and books. Their drawings demonstrate an understanding of a story and often offer insight into their feelings and interpretation of the story.

Teachers have found that "Picture Reviews" enhance children's comprehension and appreciation for books and stories.

You might begin by having the whole class complete the same version of a Picture Review after you have read a story aloud to them. Later, you may wish to supply your class with a variety of Picture Review forms from which to choose. Children will soon begin adding original comments to the forms you provide. Before long, they will be producing their own "Book Reports."

Teachers often use Picture Reviews for "Shared Picture Experiences." Children can share their reviews with the whole class at group time. This experience promotes listening and questioning skills, language development, and appreciation for others' viewpoints. After sharing time, children may take their Picture Reviews home or add them to a Picture Review Bulletin Board.

PARENTAL INVOLVEMENT

Keeping parents informed and helping them understand the activities of a whole language program (or, for that matter, any program) is very important to the success of that program.

Moreover, Picture Reviews provide natural opportunities for parents to share their children's reactions to stories and books.

Valuable language and communication skills are developed during this interaction and response to children's artwork. Children's drawings allow for meaning making in ways that might otherwise be inhibited if children are restricted to words only.

Dear Family,

Today we heard the story

_____

Ask me about my picture and the story.

Dear Family,

Today we heard the story

_____

by _____

My Favorite Character

Dear Family,

Today we heard the story

_____

by _____

The Part I Liked Best

Hello!

Let's talk about my picture.

Today I heard the story

_____

Below is a scene from the story.

Hello!

Let's talk about my pictures.

Today I heard the story

_____

Below are two scenes from the story.

Hello! Let's talk about my pictures.

Today I heard the story

_____

Below are three scenes in order from the story.

Hello!

Ask me about my picture, and I will tell you a story.

Repair Shop

_____

_____

_____

_____

_____

Repair Shop

_____

_____

_____

_____

_____

Repair Shop

_____

_____

_____

_____

_____

Repair Shop

_____

_____

_____

_____

_____

Server:

Total	

Server:

Total	

Server:

Total	

Server:

Total	

Doctor: _____

Patient: _____

Rx: _____

_____

_____

Doctor: _____

Patient: _____

Rx: _____

_____

_____

Doctor: _____

Patient: _____

Rx: _____

_____

_____

Doctor: _____

Patient: _____

Rx: _____

_____

_____

Fix-it Garage

_____

_____

_____

_____

_____

Fix-it Garage

_____

_____

_____

_____

_____

Fix-it Garage

_____

_____

_____

_____

Fix-it Garage

_____

_____

_____

_____

Vet's Office

Pet Owner: _____

Kind of Pet: _____

Rx: _____

_____

_____

Vet's Office

Pet Owner: _____

Kind of Pet: _____

Rx: _____

_____

_____

Vet's Office

Pet Owner: _____

Kind of Pet: _____

Rx: _____

_____

_____

Vet's Office

Pet Owner: _____

Kind of Pet: _____

Rx: _____

_____

_____

Recipe for

_____

_____

_____

_____

_____

Recipe for

_____

_____

_____

_____

_____

Recipe for

_____

_____

_____

_____

Recipe for

_____

_____

_____

_____

Telephone Message

To: _____

From: _____

Message:

_____

_____

_____

Telephone Message

To: _____

From: _____

Message:

_____

_____

_____

Telephone Message

To: _____

From: _____

Message:

_____

_____

_____

Telephone Message

To: _____

From: _____

Message:

_____

_____

_____

Things to Do

_____

_____

_____

_____

_____

Things to Do

_____

_____

_____

_____

_____

Things to Do

_____

_____

_____

_____

Things to Do

_____

_____

_____

_____

Observations

_____

_____

_____

_____

_____

Observations

_____

_____

_____

_____

_____

Observations

_____

_____

_____

_____

_____

Observations

_____

_____

_____

_____

_____

Invitation to Smile

_____ would

like a smile from

_____

Invitation to Smile

_____ would

like a smile from

_____

Invitation to Smile

_____ would

like a smile from

_____

Invitation to Smile

_____ would

like a smile from

_____

PHRASES

Phrases help children become comfortable exchanging written messages. The feedback they receive will encourage them to continue to use and develop their writing skills.

Phrases provide opportunities for fun exchanges through which children gain significant insights into the form, nature, and conventions of written dialogue.

HOW TO IMPLEMENT PHRASES

1. Photocopy Phrases pages from the book.

2. Read them to your class.

3. Ask children to decide on a picture for each phrase. (This enables nonreaders to use the pages independently.)

4. Place the Phrases in your writing area.

5. Provide pencils and paper for students to write notes to classmates, family, school employees, and so on. Children usually start by copying phrases, then move on to constructing their own phrases.

I want to play with you.

You make me smile.

Happy Birthday.

Your picture is nice.

I am your friend.

I love you.

Have a happy day.

I like your project.

Please write me a note.

You make me laugh.

AUTHOR PAGES

Author Pages promote feelings of importance in young writers. Children enjoy sharing information about themselves, and the information shared may serve as topics for future writings.

STUDENT PHOTO CARDS

1. Take black-and-white pictures of students. (Black-and-white pictures photocopy well.)

2. Make photocopies of class pictures.

3. Glue photographs to file cards or oaktag.

4. Cover with clear self-adhesive paper or laminate.

By having Student Photo Cards in your classroom, your students will be able to write messages to classmates on their own. Most students learn to read classmates' names very quickly and soon write them without the help of the photo cards. (Some teachers give a set of photo cards to a class monitor for taking attendance.)

About the Author

Name _____

Age _____   School _____

Picture of Author

Favorite Food

Favorite Story or Book

About the Author

Name_____

Age_____

Family Portrait

Favorite Story or Book

Best Toy

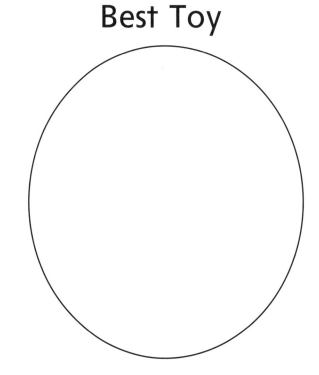

About the Author

Name_____

Birth Date _____

Favorite Food

Favorite Activity

Pets
(Real or Imaginary)

Picture of Author

Interesting Facts About the Author

Name_____

Age_____

A Game the Author Likes to Play

Favorite Holiday

Something That Makes the Author Happy

About the Author

Name _____

Age _____ Grade _____

Picture of Author

Author Playing Favorite Game

Something the Author Hopes To Write About in the Future

Interesting Facts About the Author

Name_____

Age_____

Picture of Author

Place Author Would
Most Like to Visit

Favorite Food

Activity Author Enjoys

All About the Author

Name_____

Age_____

Picture of Author

Family Portrait

Favorite Food

Favorite Book

About the Author

Name_____

Age _____   Teacher _____

Favorite Summer
Activity

Favorite Autumn
Activity

Favorite Winter
Activity

Favorite Spring
Activity

About the Author

Name _____

Favorite Activity

About the Author

Name _____

Imaginary Pet

About the Author

Name _____

Favorite Place

About the Author

Name_____

Favorite Meal

About the Author

Name_____

Favorite Story

WEEKEND NEWS

This activity encourages children to remember words and sentences that describe events that are of real interest to them and to see the purpose in recording details. Children fill in their "Weekend News" on Monday mornings and share their news with partners or with the whole group. Weekend News reports can be hung on a bulletin board or collated into a book format. (Children enjoy reading about one another's news.)

Variations include "Nightly News," " Vacation News," and "Classroom News," which enable the teacher to note what children value and remember from their daily activities and serve as informal modes of communication with parents.

Students may dictate their news to a teacher, adult, or upper-grade volunteer, or use their own invented spellings to communicate directly on paper.

Weekend News

Reporter: _____

Vacation News

_____

_____

_____

_____

_____

Reporter: _____

Classroom News

Reporter: _____